3
three

bear
swimsuit
flippers
water
fish

rucksack
nut
squirrel

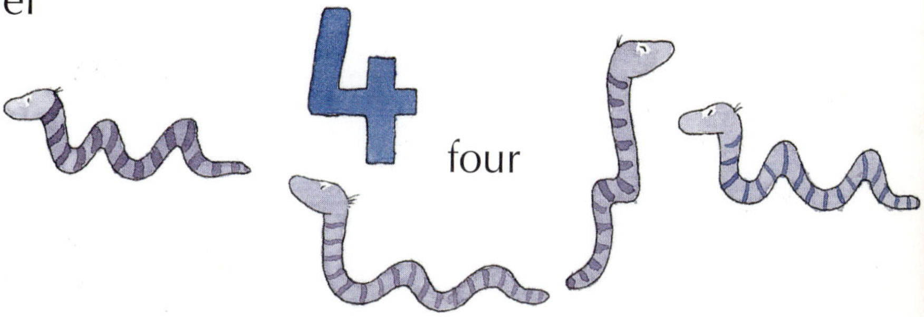
4
four

22
APRIL
calendar

stars

snail
tomato
lettuce
radish

campfire

5
five

Annet Rudolph
hat die kuscheligen Bären und ihre Freunde gemalt. Schon als Kind waren ihre Lieblingsbeschäftigungen Malen und Schmökern in Bilderbüchern. Später, nach dem Abschluß eines Grafik-Design-Studiums, hat Frau Rudolph ihr Hobby zum Beruf gemacht. Seit 1990 lebt sie in einem kleinen Dorf am Fuße der schwäbischen Alb und hat inzwischen 16 Bilder- und Liederbücher illustriert.

Leonora Fröhlich-Ward
hat sich die englischen Texte ausgedacht. Mit großer Freude bringt sie Kindern im Kindergarten und in der Grundschule die ersten englischen Wörter und Sätze bei. Es ist aber sehr wichtig für sie, daß die Kinder die Sprache beim Spielen lernen – durch Vorlesen, Nachsprechen oder Nachsingen. Denn es soll ja schließlich Spaß machen ...

99 98 97 96   5 4 3 2 1

Ausstattung und Herstellung: arsEdition, München
Umschlaggestaltung: Michael Keller
Printed in Germany
ISBN 3-7607-4644-6

Die deutsche Bibliothek – CIP-Einheitsaufnahme

Englisch mit Sue und Sam / Ill. Annet Rudolph.
Text Leonora Fröhlich-Ward. – München : Ars-Ed., 1996
Franz. Ausg. u. d. T.: Französisch mit Marie und Paul
ISBN 3-7607-4644-6
NE: Rudolph, Annet; Fröhlich-Ward, Leonora

ENGLISCH

mit Sue und Sam

Illustrationen: Annet Rudolph
Text: Leonora Fröhlich-Ward

arsEdition

An alle Erwachsenen wie Eltern, Großeltern, Tanten, Onkel, Erzieherinnen und Erzieher ...

Dieses Sprachbuch wurde für Kinder im Alter von 4 bis 8 Jahren entwickelt. In diesem Alter sind die Kinder besonders begabt, Fremdsprachen allein durch Hören und Nachsprechen fast akzentfrei zu lernen. Den Kindern bereitet das Spielen mit der Sprache viel Freude.
Wenn es den Erwachsenen gelingt, diesen Spieltrieb und die Freude beim Sprechen sinnvoll zu nutzen und rechtzeitig zu fördern, werden Sie erstaunt sein, wie schnell und mit welcher Begeisterung Ihr Kind bald englische Wörter und Sätze sprechen kann. Dieses Buch soll Sie dabei unterstützen. Die Bilder helfen, die kleinen Geschichten über die Bären Sue und Sam zu verstehen. Lesen Sie dem Kind die Dialoge und Texte vor, betrachten Sie gemeinsam die Abbildungen, und ermutigen Sie die Kinder zum Nachsprechen und -spielen der kleinen Geschichten.
Falls Sie einige Wörter oder Sätze nicht verstehen, können Sie im hinteren Teil des Buches bei den vollständigen Übersetzungen der Texte oder im Wörterverzeichnis nachschlagen. Das Wörterverzeichnis gibt Ihnen mit der Lautschrift auch Hilfen für die richtige Aussprache.
Im Englischen gibt es häufig zusammengezogene Formen: Man kann *it is* ebenso sagen wie *it's* oder *let us* wie *let's*. Beide Formen sind richtig. Die Geschichten sind im kindgemäßen Englisch geschrieben. Die Kinder lernen viele nützliche Wörter kennen, die in alltäglichen Situationen vorkommen.

Zu diesem Buch gibt es auch eine gleichnamige Toncassette (Bestellnummer 26.4645). Wenn Sie diese gemeinsam mit Ihrem Kind anhören, die Kinder nachsprechen und nachsingen lassen und dabei die Bilder betrachten, werden Sie und Ihr Kind viel Spaß haben und sich ganz nebenbei noch mehr Vokabeln merken.

Viel Spaß beim Englischlernen mit Sue, Sam und ihren Freunden!

Sue and Sam are two little bears. They will help you to learn English. We will follow them through the year. You will learn about the four seasons and the twelve months. Then you will see what the bears like doing at each time of the year.

Autumn

Here are Sue and Sam. Sam wants to go shopping.

Sue: Good morning, Sam.
Sam: Good morning, Sue. I'm going shopping. Where's my rucksack?
Sue: Your rucksack? Here it is. And here's the shopping list.
Sam: Thank you. Let's see. Nuts, apples, honey. Good, I like honey.
Sue: Oh look. It's raining, and it's windy!
Sam: Raining? Where's my umbrella?
Sue: Umbrella? Oh, no, it's too windy!
Sam: No, it isn't. I want my umbrella. Bye, bye, Sue.
Sue: Bye, bye.

Sam has finished shopping. His rucksack is full.
But ... the wind!

Rain on the green grass
And rain on the tree
And rain on the house tops
But don't rain on me.

But the wind stops and Sam stops flying!

Sam: Ooh! I'm falling, I'm falling!

Yellow, green and brown
The leaves are falling down!
If you fall on your head
They make you a soft bed.
Yellow, green and brown
The leaves are falling down.

Sam: Ouch! My head, my arm, my hand, my nose! Oh, what is it? There is something under the leaves. What is it? Hello! Who are you?

Henry: I'm Henry Hedgehog. Who are you?

Sam: I'm Sam Bear. Ouch, my nose!

Henry: Sorry. Let's be friends.

Sam: Fine, let's be friends.

Henry wants to sleep. He's tired. Sam says goodbye.

Sam: Now I must go home.
Henry: Thank you for your visit. Good night.
Sam: Good night? Do you want to go to bed?
Henry: Yes, it's time for bed. Here's my visiting card. Come and see me in April.
Sam: In April? It's October now.
Henry: Yes, I sleep from October to April
Sam: Okay, Henry. See you in April. Bye, bye. Sleep well.

Sam comes home with the shopping.

Sam:	Hello, Sue. Here I am and here's the shopping.
Sue:	Hello. Have you got the apples?
Sam:	Yes, here are the apples and the nuts and the honey.
Sue:	And what's this? A visiting card.
Sam:	Yes, it's my friend's card.
Sue:	Your friend? What's his name?
Sam:	His name is Henry Hedgehog.
Sue:	Can we visit him?
Sam:	Not today. He's sleeping. We can visit him in April. He sleeps from October to April.
Sue:	Fine. Then we can visit him in April.

Winter

This morning Sue wakes Sam up. Why ...?

Sue:	Wake up, Sam, it's snowing!
Sam:	What?
Sue:	Wake up, it's snowing!
Sam:	What? Snowing? Oh, it's feathers! It's not snowing.
Sue:	All right, all right!

Look out of the window! It is snowing!

Sue: But look! It is snowing in the garden. Look!
Sam: Hurrah! Snow, real snow. Let's go skiing.
Sue: No, not skiing. I want to make a snowman.
Sam: Where is my pullover? Where is my anorak?
Sue: Your pullover is in the cupboard. Your anorak is hanging on the cupboard.
Sam: Where are my skis?
Sue: Your skis are under the cupboard. Where are my pants?
Sam: Your pants are under the bed.

Sam is skiing and Sue is making a snowman. The sun is shining.

Sam: I like skiing! It's sunny today. I like the sun.
Sue: I like my snowman! And I like the sun.

The Snowman

Look at my snowman, round and fat.
He has got a scarf and a woolly hat!
Stones for his eyes, a carrot for his nose,
Sticks for his arms and boots for his toes.

Oh dear! Sam has fallen down. He has hurt his leg.

Sam: Ouch, my leg!
Sue: Oh! Let's go to the doctor!

Sam: I like riding on a sleigh. Thank you for pulling me.
Sue: I like pulling you. Let's go home.

The bears are having a quiet day at home.

Sam: I like the fire. It's warm!

Sue: Yes, it's cold outside, and it's snowing. How is your leg, Sam?

Sam: Fine, thank you, Sue. But I'm thirsty. May I have a drink please?

Sue: A drink? Yes, what would you like? Fruit tea or a lemon and honey drink?

Sam: Fruit tea? No, thank you. But I like lemon and honey. A lemon and honey drink, please.

Recipe: Lemon and Honey Drink

1 cup water
2 teaspoons honey
1 lemon

Heat the water.
Put 2 spoons of honey in a cup. Cut the lemon in half. Squeeze it.
Pour the juice into the cup.
Pour the hot water over the honey and the lemon juice.
Stir the drink. Mm. That's good!

Spring
March
April
May

Summer
June
July
August

Autumn
September
October
November

Winter
December
January
February

Spring

Sue and Sam are having breakfast together.
Look at the calendar – April 1!

Sue: Good morning, Sam.
Sam: Good morning, Sue, come and have your breakfast.
Sue: I'm thirsty.
Sam: Do you want tea or cocoa to drink?
Sue: Tea, please.
Sam: Here you are. Are you hungry?
Sue: Yes, I'm hungry. Where are the bearflakes?
Sam: The bearflakes? Here they are.
Sue: Oh, a bird!
Bird: April fool! Catch me!
Sue: What a surprise! A bird! Let's catch the bird!

Suddenly a bird flew through the window into the room. Sue and Sam are really surprised.
But where is the bird now? Sue and Sam are looking for it.

Sam: Is it on the cupboard?
Sue: No, it isn't.
Sam: Behind the cupboard?
Sue: No, it isn't. Look under the couch.
Sam: No, it isn't there.
Sue: Look, it's in your rucksack!
Sam: Hurrah, I've got it. Come along, let's go out.
Sue: Yes, let's go into the garden.

It is a lovely spring day. The bears and the bird are in the garden.

Sam: Could you help me sow the seeds please.
Sue: No, I want to go on the swing. The bird can help you.
Sam: Come here, bird. Please help me.
Bird: All right. Give me the seeds.
Sam: All right, first some carrots here. Thank you. Then some radishes there.
Bird: Then some beans here.

Sue is on the swing. She likes swinging.

Sue: Could you push me please, Sam?
Sam: All right, push. Up you go!
Sue: Thank you Sam. Whee. It's fun on the swing.

How do you like to go up in a swing?
Up in the air so blue?
Oh, I do think it's the pleasantest thing
Ever a child can do.

(Robert Louis Stevenson)

The bunnies want to hide their eggs in the garden. Sue, Sam and Henry Hedgehog are helping them.

Bunny: Hello, Sue and Sam. We want to hide the eggs!
Sam: Can we help you?
Sue: Yes, let's hide a red egg under the bush.
Bunny: A blue egg behind the flowers.
Sam: An orange egg next to the beans.
Henry: A yellow egg and a purple egg in the grass.

Bunny:	And another yellow egg under the tree.
Henry:	An orange egg under the swing.
Sue:	A purple egg in the flowers.
Sam:	And a red egg in the tree, in the bird's nest.
Bunnies:	Ooh, yes. Up in the tree! Here's an empty nest.
Sue:	That's a good idea!
Sam:	Up you go, Henry.
Bunnies:	Finished! Thank you, everybody.
Sue:	Hurrah, the baskets are empty!

Summer

Sue and Sam are at the campsite. They want to go swimming. Henry comes to visit them.

Sue: There! Our tent is up! Now, where is my swimsuit?
Sam: Here's mine – but where are my sunglasses?
Sue: And my flippers? And my suncream?
Henry: Hello, Sam, what are you doing here?
Sam: Oh, hello, Henry. We're camping.
Sue: Do you like swimming, Henry? We're going swimming.
Henry: No, I don't like swimming, but I can come and watch you.
Sue: Okay, let's go. And then we'll have a picnic.
Henry: All right. I like picnics.

After swimming the bears and Henry are hungry.
They like picnics. They don't like bees.

Sue: I'm hungry now. Let's have a picnic.
Sam: And I'm thirsty. I want something to drink. What have you got, Sue?
Sue: Fruit tea and lemonade.
Sam: Oh no! Not fruit tea! I want lemonade.
Sue: I've got some tomatoes and a cheese sandwich. And two honey sandwiches, and three apples. What do you want, Henry?
Henry: I like apples. An apple, please.
Sue: And you, Sam?
Sam: A cheese sandwich, please. I like cheese. Thank you.
Sue: And I like tomatoes. Ooh, a bee. Go away.
Henry: Go away, bee. I don't like bees.

I'm a bee, can't you see,
I'm a busy, busy bee!
I like honey and I like tea.
I'm a busy, busy bee!

Sam likes fishing but Henry and Sue want to play mini-golf.

Sue: Let's play mini-golf.
Sam: No, I want to go fishing. I want a fish for supper.
Henry: But I like mini-golf. I can play with you, Sue.
Sue: Come on Henry, you can start. Here is the ball. First we go through the tunnel.
Henry: One ...! Two ... through the tunnel. Three ... in the hole! Hurrah!
Sue: Good, now it's my turn. One, two ... in the hole!
Henry: You're very good. Now let's try the next one. Up the hill.
Sue: Try again, Henry.
Henry: There! Up the hill. Hurrah. It's in the hole. Now it's your turn, Sue.
Sue: All right, up the hill. One ..., two ..., three ..., four ...! Hurrah, it's in the hole.

Henry: All right. Now down the hill. It's my turn.
Sue: Oh dear! The ball is in the water!
Let's go and see Sam.

1, 2, 3, 4, 5, once I caught a fish alive,
6, 7, 8, 9, 10, then I let it go again.
Why did you let it go?
Because it bit my finger so!
Which finger did it bite?
This little finger on the right!

In the evening Sam, Sue and Henry are sitting around the campfire. The fish is cooking on the fire.

Sue:	That's a big fish, Sam. I'm hungry.
Henry:	Fish for supper. I like fish. I like camping.
Sue:	Yes, camping is fun. Hey, look at the stars.
Sam:	I can sing you a song about the stars.

Twinkle, twinkle, little star,
How I wonder what you are.
Up above the world so high
Like a diamond in the sky.
Twinkle, twinkle, little star,
How I wonder what you are.

The bears are tired. It was a lovely day. The moon and the stars are shining.
Good night everybody.

Sam: I'm tired. That was a lovely day.
Sue: Yes, I'm tired too. That fish was very good, Sam.
Sam: Where's my sleeping bag?
Sue: In the tent. Look at the moon. It's shining.
Sam: Yes, it's lovely. Henry, are you tired? ... Henry?
Henry: Yes. Good night, everybody. Sleep well.
Sue: Sleep well. Good night.

Tips zur englischen Aussprache

Um die englische Aussprache von Anfang an richtig zu lernen, ist es natürlich das Beste, so oft wie möglich Leuten zuzuhören, die Englisch als Muttersprache sprechen, z. B. auf Reisen oder im Radio. Du wirst schnell feststellen, daß einige Laute anders klingen als im Deutschen. Die Sprachmelodie (Intonation) ist teilweise auch nicht die gleiche.
Damit du selbst nachsehen kannst, wie ein Wort richtig ausgesprochen wird, haben wir im Wörterverzeichnis (ab S. 35) eine Lautschrift hinter die englischen Wörter gesetzt. Schau dir die nachfolgenden Symbole genau an: Es ist gar nicht schwierig, die Lautschrift lesen zu lernen.

[ˈ] vor der betonten Silbe eines Worts steht ein Apostroph:

breakfast	ˈbrekfəst	Frühstück

[iː] zwei Punkte hinter einem Vokal (Selbstlaut) bedeuten, daß dieser lang gesprochen wird, wie das **ie** in »Schiene«:

bee	biː	Biene
fruit	fruːt	Obst, Frucht

Vokale

[ʌ] spricht man mit auseinandergezogenen Lippen. Es hört sich an wie ein Laut zwischen **o** und **a**:

but	bʌt	aber

[ə] sprichst du wie das **e** am Ende von deutschen Wörtern, z. B. »Tante«, »Frage« oder »Dose«:

summer	ˈsʌmə	Sommer

[ɛə] ist eine Kombination aus einem halblang gesprochenen **ä** und einem unbetonten **e**:

bear	bɛə	Bär

[æ] gibt es als Laut im Deutschen nicht. Es wird etwa gesprochen wie **ä** in »Ähre«, allerdings etwas kürzer; der Mund ist dabei weit geöffnet:

anorak	ˈænəræk	Anorak
cat	kæt	Katze

[ei] klingt wie das lange **e** in »See« und dahinter ein kurzes **i**:

make	meik	machen

[ai] sprichst du wie **ai** in »Mai« (das **i** kann man gerade noch hören):

I	ai	ich
to **fly**	flai	fliegen

[au] klingt wie das **au** in »aua«:

house	haus	Haus

[ɔ] ist ein offenes, kurzes **o** wie in »noch«:

hot	hɔt	heiß

[ou] klingt wie das **o** in »Opa«, dem ein kurzes **u** folgt:

no	nou	nein
over	ˈouvə	über

[i] klingt wie das kurze **i** in »singen«:

to **give**	giv	geben

[u] sprichst du wie das kurze **u** in »Kutsche«:

to **put**	put	stellen

Konsonanten

Die Konsonanten (Mitlaute) **b, d, f, h, k, m, n, p, q, s, t** und **x** werden im Englischen genauso wie im Deutschen gesprochen.

[g] spricht man wie **g** in »Geld«:

good	gud	gut

[ʒ] sprichtst du wie ein weiches **sch** in »Journal«:

June	dʒuːn	Juni

[l] hört sich anders an als im Deutschen. Die Zunge ist leicht gerollt und liegt vorne am Gaumen:

flower	ˈflauə	Blume

[ŋ] hört sich an wie der Nasenlaut in »singen«:

thing	ðiŋ	Ding

[r] klingt im Englischen auch anders und wird nur vor Vokalen (Selbstlauten) gesprochen. Roll deine Zungenspitze nach hinten an den Gaumen:

red	red	rot

[ʃ] klingt wie **sch** in »Schnee«:

fish	fiʃ	Fisch

[ð] ist ein »Zungenbrecher«, den du ein bißchen üben mußt! Es ist ein Zeichen für das englische **th** und klingt wie ein gelispeltes deutsches **s**. Du sprichst es mit der Zunge zwischen den Zähnen:

the	ðə	der, die, das
this	ðis	dies

[v] sprichst du wie den Anfangsbuchstaben in »Welt« oder »Ventil«:

visit	ˈvizit	Besuch

[w] Hier sind die Lippen fast geschlossen und gerundet wie beim **u**, als ob du etwas wegblasen willst. Es klingt aber nicht wie das deutsche **w** oder **v**:

window	windou	Fenster

[z] wird wie das **s** in »bremsen« gesprochen:

zoo	zuː	Zoo

Englisch-Deutsch

A

a	ei/ə	ein(e)	7 ff.
about	ə'baut	über	7, 32
above	ə'bʌv	über	32
after	'a:ftə	nach	29
again	ə'gen	wieder, noch einmal	31
air	ɛə	Luft	25
alive	ə'laiv	lebend	31
all right	'ɔ:l'rait	in Ordnung	14
am	æm	bin	
I am/I'm		ich bin	11,29
and	ænd	und	7
anorak	'ænəræk	Anorak	15
apple	'æpl	Apfel	2, 8
April	'eiprəl	April	12
April Fool!		April! April!	22
are	a:	sind, seid	7, 8 ff.
arm	a:m	Arm	11
around	ə'raund	um, herum	32
at	æt	zu	18
August	'ɔ:gəst	August	20
Autumn	'ɔ:təm	Herbst	8

B

ball	bɔ:l	Ball	30
basket	'ba:skit	Korb	27
to **be**	bi:	sein	7 ff.
it is (it's)		es ist	7, 8 ff.
bean	bi:n	Bohne	26
bear	bɛə	Bär	7
bearflakes	bɛə'fleiks	»Bärenflocken«	22
bed	bed	Bett	10
bee	bi:	Biene	29
behind	bi'haind	hinter, dahinter	23
big	big	groß	32
bird	bə:d	Vogel	2, 22
to **bite**	bait	beißen	31
he, she, it bit		er, sie, es biß	31
blue	blu:	blau	25
book	'buk	Buch	2
boot	bu:t	Stiefel	16
breakfast	'brekfəst	Frühstück	22
brown	braun	braun	10
bush	buʃ	Busch, Strauch	26
busy	'bizi	beschäftigt	29
but	bʌt	aber	9
bye bye!	bai'bai	Auf Wiedersehen!	8

C

calendar	'kæləndə	Kalender	22
campfire	'kæmp'faiə	Lagerfeuer	32
campsite	'kæmp'sait	Zeltplatz	28
carrot	'kærət	Karotte, Möhre	16
cat	kæt	Katze	2
to **catch**	kætʃ	fangen	22
I caught		ich fing	31
cheese	tʃi:z	Käse	29
cocoa	kɔkɔ	Kakao	22
cold	kould	kalt	18
to **come**	kʌm	kommen	12
he, she, it comes		er, sie, es kommt	13
couch	kautʃ	Sofa	23
cupboard	'kʌbəd	Schrank	15
to **cut**	kʌt	schneiden	19

D

diamond	'daiəmənd	Diamant	32
to **do**	du:	tun, machen	12, 25, 28
don't		nicht tun	9
doctor	'dɔktə	Arzt	17
down	daun	nach unten	10
drink	driŋk	Getränk	18
to **drink**	driŋk	trinken	18, 19, 22

E

each	i:tʃ	jede (r, s)	7
empty	'empti	leer	27
English	'iŋgliʃ	Englisch	7
evening	'i:vniŋ	Abend	32
ever	'evə	immer	25
everybody	'evribɔdi	jeder, alle	33
eye	ai	Auge	16

F

to **fall**	fɔ:l	fallen	10
I'm falling		ich falle gerade	10
fat	fæt	dick	16
feather	'feðə	Feder	14
February	'februri	Februar	21
fine	fain	fein, gut	18
finger	'fiŋə	Finger	31
finished	'finiʃt	beendet	9
fire	'faiə	Feuer	18
first	fə:st	zuerst	24
fish	fiʃ	Fisch	30
to **fish**	fiʃ	fischen, angeln	30
five	faiv	fünf	9
flippers	flipəs	Schwimmflossen	28
flower	'flauə	Blume	26
to **fly**	flai	fliegen	10
a bird flew		ein Vogel flog	23
to **follow**	'fɔlou	folgen	7

for	fɔ:	für	12
four	fɔ:	vier	8
friend	frend	Freund	11
from ... to ...	frɔm ... tu: ...	von ... bis ...	12
fruit	fru:t	Obst, Frucht	18
full	ful	voll	9
fun	fʌn	Spaß	32

G

garden	'ga:dn	Garten	15
to **give**	giv	geben	24
to **go away**	gou ə'wei	weggehen	29
good	gud	gut	8, 27
Good morning!		Guten Morgen!	8
Good night!		Gute Nacht!	12
grass	gra:s	Gras	9
green	gri:n	grün	9

H

half	ha:f	Hälfte	19
hand	hænd	Hand	11
to **hang**	'hæŋ	hängen	15
hat	hæt	Hut, Mütze	16
to **have**	hæv	haben	13
he, she, it has		er, sie, es hat	16
head	hed	Kopf	10
to **heat**	hi:t	erwärmen	19
hedgehog	'hedʒhɔg	Igel	2, 11
hello!	hə'lou	Hallo!	11
to **help**	help	helfen	7, 24
here	hir	hier	8
to **hide**	haid	verstecken	26
high	hai	hoch	32
hill	hil	Hügel	30
hole	houl	Loch	30
home	houm	Heim, Haus	12
honey	'hʌni	Honig	8
hot	hɔt	heiß	19
house	haus	Haus	9
house top	haus tɔp	hier: Dach	9
how	hau	wie	18
hungry	'hʌŋri	hungrig	22
hurrah!	hu'ra:	Hurra!	15

I

I	ai	ich	8
idea	ai'diə	Idee	27
if	if	wenn, falls	10
in	in	in	7 ff.
into	'intu	in, hinein	23, 32
is (to be)	iz	ist (sein)	8 ff.
it	it	es	8 ff.
it is not/it isn't		es ist nicht	8

J

January	'dʒænjuəri	Januar	21
July	'dʒu:'lai	Juli	20
June	dʒu:n	Juni	20

L

leaf	li:f	Blatt	11
(Plural: leaves)		(Mehrzahl: Blätter)	
to **learn**	lə:n	lernen	7
leg	leg	Bein	17
lemon	'lemən	Zitrone	18
lemonade	'lemə'neid	Limonade	29
to **let**	let	lassen	8
lettuce	letis	Kopfsalat	7
to **like**	laik	mögen, gern haben	7
list	list	Liste	8
little	'litl	klein	7
to **look**	luk	sehen	8
to look out of		hinaussehen	15
lovely	'lʌvli	wundervoll	24

M

to **make**	meik	machen	10
to make a snowman		einen Schneemann bauen	16
March	ma:tʃ	März	20
May	mei	Mai	20
me	mi:	mich, mir	9
mini-golf	'mini-gɔlf	Minigolf	30
month	mʌnð	Monat	7
moon	mu:n	Mond	33
morning	'mɔ:niŋ	Morgen	14
my	mai	mein	8
it's my turn		ich bin an der Reihe	30

N

name	neim	Name	13
nest	nest	Nest	27
next	nekst	nächste (r, s)	30
next to		neben	26
night	nait	Nacht	12
nine	nain	neun	31
no	nou	nein	8
no, it isn't		nein, es ist nicht	23
nose	nouz	Nase	11
not	nɔt	nicht	13
November	nou'vembə	November	21
now	nau	jetzt	12
nut	nʌt	Nuß	8

O

October	ɔk'toubə	Oktober	12
okay	'ou'kei	in Ordnung	12

on	ɔn	auf	9
once	wʌns	einst	31
one	wʌn	eins	2
or	ɔ:	oder	22
orange	ˈɔrindʒ	orange(farben)	26
Ouch!	autʃ	Aua!	11
out	aut	aus	15
outside	ˈautsaid	draußen	18
over	ˈouvə	über	19
P			
pants	pænts	Hose	15
picnic	ˈpiknik	Picknick	28
pillow	ˈpilou	Kissen	14
to **play**	plei	spielen	30
the **pleasantest** thing	plezntest	die schönste Sache	25
please	pli:z	bitte	18
to **pour**	pɔ:	gießen	19
to **pull**	pul	ziehen	17
pullover	pulˈouvə	Pullover	15
purple	ˈpə:pl	lila	26
to **push**	puʃ	schieben, stoßen	25
to **put**	put	geben	19
Q			
quiet	ˈkwaiət	ruhig	18
R			
radish	ˈrædiʃ	Radieschen	24
rain	rein	Regen	9
it's raining		es regnet	8
recipe	ˈresipi	Rezept	19
red	red	rot	26
to **ride**	raid	fahren, reiten	17
to ride on a sleigh		Schlitten fahren	17
right	rait	rechts	31
round	raund	rund	16
rucksack	ˈrʌksæk	Rucksack	8
S			
sandwich	ˈsænwidʒ	belegtes Brot	29
scarf	sca:f	Schal	16
season	ˈsi:zn	Jahreszeit	7
to **see**	si:	sehen	12
seed	si:d	Samen	24
September	sepˈtembə	September	21
to **shine**	ʃain	scheinen, leuchten	16
to go **shopping**	ˈʃɔpiŋ	einkaufen gehen	13
shopping list	ˈʃɔpiŋ list	Einkaufsliste	8
to **sing**	siŋ	singen	32
to **sit**	sit	sitzen	32
to **ski**	ski:	Ski fahren	16

ski	ski:	Ski	15
to **sleep**	sli:p	schlafen	12
Sleep well!		Schlafe gut!	12
sleeping bag	ˈsli:piŋ bæg	Schlafsack	33
sleigh	slei	Schlitten	2, 17
snowman	snouˈmæn	Schneemann	16
so	sou	so	31
soft	sɔft	weich	10
some	sʌm	einige	29
something	sʌmðiŋ	etwas	29
song	sɔŋ	Lied	32
Sorry!	ˈsɔri	Entschuldigung! Das tut mir leid!	11
to **sow**	sou	säen	24
spoon	spu:n	Löffel	19
spring	spriŋ	Frühling	20
star	sta:	Stern	32
to **start**	sta:t	anfangen	30
stick	stik	Stock, Zweig	16
to **stir**	stə:	umrühren	19
stone	stoun	Stein	16
to **stop**	stɔp	aufhören	10
summer	ˈsʌmə	Sommer	20
sun	sʌn	Sonne	16
suncream	sʌnkri:m	Sonnencreme	28
sunglasses	sʌngla:ses	Sonnenbrille	28
sunny	ˈsʌni	sonnig	16
it's sunny		es ist sonnig	16
supper	ˈsʌpə	Abendessen	32
surprise	səˈpraiz	Überraschung	22
to **swim**	swim	schwimmen	28
swimsuit	swimsu:t	Badeanzug	28
to **swing**	swiŋ	schaukeln	24
T			
tea	ti:	Tee	18
ten	ten	zehn	14
tent	tent	Zelt	28
thank you	ðæŋkˈju:	ich danke dir	8
the	ðə	der, die, das	7ff.
their	ðɛə	ihr (e)	26
them	ðəm	ihnen	7ff.
there	ðɛə	dort	23
they	ðei	sie	7
thing	ðiŋ	Ding, Sache	25
thirsty	ˈðə:sti	durstig	18
this	ðis	dies	13
three	ðri:	drei	7
through	ðru:	durch	7
time	taim	Zeit	7, 12
tired	ˈtaied	müde	12
to	tu:	zu	8
today	təˈdei	heute	13

toe	tou	Zeh(e)	16
together	təˈgeðə	zusammen	22
tomato	təˈma:tou	Tomate	29
too	tu:	zu, allzu	8
top	tɔp	ober(st)es Ende, hier: Dach	9
tree	tri:	Baum	9
tunnel	ˈtʌnl	Tunnel	30
twelve	twelv	zwölf	7
twinkle	ˈtwiŋkl	funkeln	32
two	tu:	zwei	7
U			
umbrella	ʌmˈbrelə	Schirm	8
under	ˈʌndə	unter	11
up	ʌp	hinauf, nach oben	25
V			
very	ˈveri	sehr	33
visit	ˈvizit	Besuch	12
to **visit**	ˈvizit	besuchen	13
visiting card	ˈvizitiŋ ka:d	Visitenkarte	12
W			
to **wake up**	weik ʌp	aufwecken	14
to **want**	wɔnt	brauchen, wollen, wünschen	12
he, she, it wants		er, sie, es will	8
warm	wɔ:m	warm	18
was (to be)	wɔz	war (sein)	33
to **watch**	wɔtʃ	beobachten, ansehen, zusehen	28
water	wɔ:tə	Wasser	19
we	wi:	wir	13
what	wɔt	was	11
where	wɛə	wo	8
who	hu:	wer	11
why	wai	warum	14
wind	wind	Wind	9
window	windou	Fenster	15
windy	ˈwindi	windig	8
it's windy		es ist windig	8
winter	ˈwintə	Winter	14
with	wið	mit	13
woolly	wuli	wollig	16
world	wə:ld	Welt	32
Y			
year	jiə:	Jahr	7
yellow	ˈjelou	gelb	10
yes	jes	ja	12
you	ju:	du, ihr, Sie	7
your	jɔ:	dein, euer	8

Deutsch-Englisch

A			
Abend	evening	ˈi:vniŋ	32
Abendessen	supper	ˈsʌpə	32
aber	but	bʌt	9
alle	everybody	ˈevribɔdi	33
anfangen	to start	sta:t	30
angeln	to fish	fiʃ	30
Anorak	anorak	ˈænəræk	15
Apfel	apple	ˈæpl	8
April	April	ˈeiprəl	12
April! April!	April Fool!		22
Arm	arm	a:m	11
Arzt	doctor	ˈdɔktə	17
Aua!	Ouch!	autʃ	11
auf	on	ɔn	9
Auf Wiedersehen!	Bye, bye!	baiˈbai	8
aufhören	to stop	stɔp	10
aufwecken	to wake up	weik ʌp	14
Auge	eye	ai	16
August	August	ˈɔ:gəst	20
aus	out	aut	15
B			
Badeanzug	swimsuit	swimsu:t	28
Ball	ball	bɔ:l	30
Bär	bear	bɛə	7
»Bärenflocken«	bearflakes	bɛəˈfleiks	22
Baum	tree	tri:	9
beenden	to finish	ˈfiniʃ	9, 27
beendet	finished	ˈfiniʃt	9
er hat beendet	he has finished		9
Bein	leg	leg	17
beißen	to bite	bait	31
er, sie, es biß	he, she, it bit		31
belegtes Brot	sandwich	ˈsænwidʒ	29
beobachten	to watch	wɔtʃ	28
beschäftigt	busy	ˈbizi	29
Besuch	visit	ˈvizit	12
besuchen	to visit	ˈvizit	13
Bett	bed	bed	10
Biene	bee	bi:	29
ich **bin**	I am	æm	11, 29
bitte	please	pli:z	18
Blatt	leaf	li:f	11
(Mehrz.: Blätter)	(Plural: leaves)		
blau	blue	blu:	25
Blume	flower	ˈflauə	26
Bohne	bean	bi:n	26
brauchen	to want	wɔnt	12

braun	brown	braun	10
Buch	book	'buk	2
Busch, Strauch	bush	buʃ	26

D

dahinter	behind	bihaind	23
danke	thank you	ðæŋk'ju:	8
das	the	ðə	7 ff.
dein, euer	your	jə:	8
der	the	ðə	7 ff.
Diamant	diamond	'daiəmənd	32
dick	fat	fæt	16
die	the	ðə	7 ff.
dies	this	ðis	13
Ding	thing	ðiŋ	25
dort	there	ðɛə	23
draußen	outside	'autsaid	18
drei	three	ðri:	7
du	you	ju:	7 ff.
durch	through	ðru:	7
durstig	thirsty	'ðə:sti	18

E

ein(e)	a	ei/ə	7 ff.
einige	some	sʌm	29
einkaufen (gehen)	(to go) shopping	'ʃɔpiŋ	13
Einkaufsliste	shopping list	'ʃɔpiŋ list	8
eins	one	wʌn	31
einst	once	wʌns	31
Englisch	English	'iŋgliʃ	7
Entschuldigung! Das tut mir leid!	Sorry!	'sɔri	11
erwärmen	to heat	hi:t	19
es	it	it	8 ff.
etwas	something	sʌmðiŋ	29
euer	your	jə:	8

F

fahren, reiten	to ride	raid	17
fallen	to fall	fɔ:l	10
falls	if	if	10
fangen	to catch	kætʃ	31
ich fing	I caught		31
Februar	February	'februri	21
Feder	feather	'feðə	14
fein, gut	fine	fain	18
Fenster	window	windou	15
Feuer	fire	'faiə	18
Finger	finger	'fiŋə	31
Fisch	fish	fiʃ	30
fischen	to fish	fiʃ	30
fliegen	to fly	flai	10
folgen	to follow	'fɔlou	7
freilassen	to let go	let gou	31
Hast du ihn freigelassen?	Did you let it go?		31
Freund	friend	frend	11
Frühling	spring	spriŋ	20
Frühstück	breakfast	'brekfəst	22
fünf	five	faiv	9
funkeln	to twinkle	'twiŋkl	32
für	for	fɔ:	12

G

Garten	garden	'ga:dn	15
geben	to give, to put	giv, put	19
gehen	to go	gou	12
weggehen	to go away		29
gelb	yellow	'jelou	10
gern haben	to like	laik	7
Getränk	drink	driŋk	18
gießen	to pour	pɔ:	19
Gras	grass	gra:s	9
groß	big	big	32
grün	green	gri:n	9
gut	fine, good	fain, gud	18, 27
Guten Morgen!	Good morning!		8
Gute Nacht!	Good night!		12

H

haben	to have	hæv	13
er, sie, es hat	he, she, it has		16
Hälfte	half	ha:f	19
hallo	hello	hə'lou	11
Hand	hand	hænd	11
hängen	to hang	'hæŋ	15
Haus	house, home	haus, houm	9, 12
Heim, Haus	home	houm	12
heiß	hot	hɔt	19
helfen	to help	help	24
sie helfen gerade	they are helping		26
Herbst	autumn	'ɔ:təm	8
herum	around	ə'raund	32
heute	today	tə'dei	13
hier	here	hiə	8
hinauf	up	ʌp	25
hinein	into	'intu	23
hinter	behind	bi'haind	23
hoch	high	hai	32
Honig	honey	'hʌni	8
Hose	pants	pænts	15
Hügel	hill	hil	30
hungrig	hungry	'hʌŋri	22
Bist du hungrig?	Are you hungry?		22
Hurra!	hurrah!	hu'ra:	15
Hut	hat	hæt	16

I

ich	I	ai	8
Idee	idea	ai'diə	27
Igel	hedgehog	'hedʒhɔg	11
ihnen	them	ðəm	7ff.
ihr	their	ðɛə	26
immer	ever	'evə	25
in	in	in	7ff.
in Ordnung	all right,	'ɔ:l'rait	14
	okay	'ou'kei	12
ist (sein)	is (to be)	iz	8ff.
es ist	it is/it's		8
es ist nicht	it is not/it isn't		8

J

ja	yes	jes	12
Jahr	year	jiə:	7
Jahreszeit	season	'si:zn	7
Januar	January	'dʒænjuəri	21
jede (r, s)	each	i:tʃ	7
jeder	everybody	'evribɔdi	33
jetzt	now	nau	12
Juli	July	'dʒu:'lai	20
Juni	June	dʒu:n	20

K

Kakao	cocoa	kɔkɔ	22
Kalender	calendar	'kæləndə	22
kalt	cold	kould	18
Karotte	carrot	'kærət	16
Käse	cheese	tʃi:z	29
Katze	cat	kæt	2
Kissen	pillow	'pilou	14
klein	little	'litl	7
kommen	to come	kʌm	12
er, sie, es kommt	he, she, it comes		13
Kopf	head	hed	10
Kopfsalat	lettuce	letis	7
Korb	basket	'ba:skit	27

L

Lagerfeuer	campfire	'kæmp'faiə	32
lassen	to let	let	8
lebend	alive	ə'laiv	31
leer	empty	'empti	27
lernen	to learn	lə:n	7
leuchten	to shine	ʃain	16
Lied	song	sɔŋ	32
lila	purple	'pə:pl	26
Limonade	lemonade	'lemə'neid	29
Liste	list	list	8
Loch	hole	houl	30
Löffel	spoon	spu:n	19
Luft	air	ɛə	25

M

machen	to make	meik	10
Mai	May	mei	20
März	March	ma:tʃ	20
mein	my	mai	8
mich	me	mi:	9
Minigolf	mini-golf	'mini-gɔlf	30
mit	with	wið	13
mögen	to like	laik	7
Möhre	carrot	'kærət	16
Monat	month	mʌnð	7
Mond	moon	mu:n	33
Morgen	morning	'mɔ:niŋ	14
müde	tired	'taied	12
Mütze	hat	hæt	16

N

nach	after	'a:ftə	29
nach oben	up	ʌp	25
nach unten	down	daun	10
nächste (r, s)	next	nekst	30
Nacht	night	nait	12
Name	name	neim	13
Nase	nose	nouz	11
neben	next to	nekst tu:	26
nein	no	nou	8ff.
nein, es ist nicht	no, it isn't		23
Nest	nest	nest	27
neun	nine	nain	31
nicht	not	nɔt	13
noch einmal	again	ə'gen	31
November	November	nou'vembə	21
Nuß	nut	nʌt	8

O

ober(st)es Ende, hier: Dach	top	tɔp	9
Obst, Frucht	fruit	fru:t	18
oder	or	ɔ:	22
Oktober	October	ɔk'toubə	12
orange(farben)	orange	'ɔrindʒ	26

P

Picknick	picnic	'piknik	28
Pullover	pullover	pul'ouvə	15

R

Radieschen	radish	'rædiʃ	24
rechts	right	rait	31
Regen	rain	rein	9
regnen	to rain	rein	9

Rezept	recipe	'resipi	19
rot	red	red	26
Rucksack	rucksack	'rʌksæk	8
ruhig	quiet	'kwaiət	18
rund	round	raund	16

S

Sache	thing	ðiŋ	25
säen	to sow	sou	24
Samen	seed	si:d	24
Schal	scarf	sca:f	16
schaukeln	to swing	swiŋ	24
scheinen	to shine	ʃain	16
Schirm	umbrella	ʌm'brelə	8
schlafen	to sleep	sli:p	12
Schlafe gut!	Sleep well!		12
Schlafsack	sleeping bag	'sli:piŋ bæg	33
Schlitten	sleigh	slei	17
Schlitten fahren	to ride on a sleigh		17
Schneemann	snowman	snou'mæn	16
einen Schneemann bauen	to make a snowman		16
schneiden	to cut	kʌt	19
Schrank	cupboard	'kʌbəd	15
schwimmen	to swim	swim	28
Schwimmflossen	flippers	flipəs	28
sehen	to look, to see	luk, si:	8, 12
hinaussehen	to look out of		15
zusehen	to watch		28
sehr	very	'veri	33
sein	to be	bi:	7ff.
September	September	sep'tembə	21
sie	they	ðəi	7ff.
sind (sein)	are (to be)	a:	7ff.
sie sind	they are		23
singen	to sing	siŋ	32
sitzen	to sit	sit	32
sie sitzen gerade	they are sitting		32
Ski	ski	ski:	15
Ski fahren	to ski	ski:	16
so	so	sou	31
Sofa	couch	kautʃ	23
Sommer	summer	'sʌmə	20
Sonne	sun	sʌn	16
Sonnenbrille	sunglasses	sʌngla:ses	28
Sonnencreme	suncream	sʌnkri:m	28
sonnig	sunny	'sʌni	16
Spaß	fun	fʌn	32
spielen	to play	plei	30
Stein	stone	stoun	16
Stern	star	sta:	32
Stiefel	boot	bu:t	16
Stock	stick	stik	16
stoßen	to push	puʃ	25
Strauch	bush	buʃ	26
suchen	to look for	luk fɔ:	23

T

Tee	tea	ti:	18
Tomate	tomato	tə'ma:tou	29
trinken	to drink	driŋk	22
tun	to do	du:	12, 25 ff.
Tunnel	tunnel	'tʌnl	30

U

über	about,	ə'baut	7, 32
	above,	ə'bʌv	32
	over	'ouvə	19
Überraschung	surprise	sə'praiz	22
um (herum)	around	ə'raund	32
umrühren	to stir	stə:	19
und	and	ænd	7
unter	under	'ʌndə	11

V

verstecken	to hide	haid	26
vier	four	fɔ:	8
Visitenkarte	visiting card	'vizitiŋ ka:d	12
Vogel	bird	bə:d	22
voll	full	ful	9
von ... bis	from ... to	frɔm ... tu: ...	12

W

war (sein)	was (to be)	wɔz	33
es war	it was		33
warm	warm	wɔ:m	18
warum	why	wai	14
was	what	wɔt	11
Wasser	water	wɔ:tə	19
weich	soft	sɔft	10
Welt	world	wə:ld	32
wenn	if	if	10
wer	who	hu:	11
wie	how	hau	18
wieder	again	ə'gen	31
Wind	wind	wind	9
windig	windy	'windi	8
Winter	winter	'wintə	14
wir	we	wi:	13
wo	where	wεə	8
wollen	to want	wɔnt	12
er, sie will	he, she wants		8
wollig	woolly	wuli	16
wundervoll	lovely	'lʌvli	24
wünschen	to want	wɔnt	12

Z			
Zeh(e)	toe	tou	16
zehn	ten	ten	14
Zeit	time	taim	12
Zelt	tent	tent	28
Zeltplatz	campsite	'kæmp'sait	28
ziehen	to pull	pul	17
Zitrone	lemon	lemən	18
zu	at	æt	18
zu Hause	at home		18
zu	to, too	tu:	8
zuerst	first	fə:st	24
zusammen	together	tə'geðə	22
zwei	two	tu:	7
Zweig	stick	stik	16
zwölf	twelve	twelv	7

Übersetzungen

Seite 7 Sue und Sam sind zwei kleine Bären. Sie werden dir dabei helfen, Englisch zu lernen. Wir werden sie durch das Jahr begleiten. Du wirst die vier Jahreszeiten und die zwölf Monate kennenlernen. Und du wirst sehen, was die Bären in den verschiedenen Zeiten des Jahres am liebsten tun.

Seite 8 Herbst
Hier sind Sue und Sam. Sam möchte einkaufen gehen.

Sue: Guten Morgen Sam.
Sam: Guten Morgen Sue. Ich gehe einkaufen. Wo ist mein Rucksack?
Sue: Dein Rucksack? Hier ist er. Und hier ist die Einkaufsliste.
Sam: Danke. Laß mal sehen. Nüsse, Äpfel, Honig. Gut, ich mag Honig.
Sue: O, schau. Es regnet, und es ist windig!
Sam: Es regnet! Wo ist mein Regenschirm?
Sue: Regenschirm? O nein, es ist zu windig!
Sam: Nein, ist es nicht. Ich möchte meinen Regenschirm. Auf Wiedersehen, Sue.
Sue: Auf Wiedersehen.

Seite 9 Sam hat eingekauft. Sein Rucksack ist voll. Aber ... der Wind!

Regne auf das grüne Gras
Und regne auf den Baum
Und regne auf die Dächer
Aber regne nicht auf mich.

Sam: Hui! Ich fliege! Ich fliege gern!

Seite 10 Aber der Wind läßt nach, und Sam kann nicht mehr fliegen!

Sam: Ooh! Ich falle, ich falle!

Gelb, grün und braun
Die Blätter fallen herab!
Wenn du auf den Kopf fällst
Bereiten sie dir ein weiches Bett.
Gelb, grün und braun
Die Blätter fallen herab.

Seite 11 Sam: Autsch! Mein Kopf, mein Arm, meine Hand, meine Nase! Oh, was ist das? Da ist etwas unter den Blättern. Was ist das? Hallo! Wer bist du?
Henry: Ich bin Henry Igel. Wer bist du?

Sam: Ich bin Sam Bär. Autsch, meine Nase!
Henry: Das tut mir leid. Laß uns Freunde sein.
Sam: Fein, laß uns Freunde sein.

Seite 12 Henry möchte schlafen. Er ist müde. Sam verabschiedet sich.

Sam: Nun muß ich nach Hause gehen.
Henry: Danke für deinen Besuch. Gute Nacht.
Sam: Gute Nacht? Willst du ins Bett gehen?
Henry: Ja, es ist Zeit zu schlafen. Hier ist meine Visitenkarte. Komme mich im April wieder besuchen.
Sam: Im April? Wir haben jetzt Oktober.
Henry: Ja, ich schlafe von Oktober bis April.
Sam: In Ordnung, Henry. Bis April. Auf Wiedersehen. Schlafe gut.

Seite 13 Sam kommt nach Hause mit den Dingen, die er eingekauft hat.

Sam: Hallo, Sue. Hier bin ich, und das habe ich eingekauft.
Sue: Hallo. Hast du die Äpfel?
Sam: Ja, hier sind die Äpfel und die Nüsse und der Honig.
Sue: Und was ist das? Eine Visitenkarte.
Sam: Ja, das ist die Karte von meinen Freund.
Sue: Dein Freund? Wie heißt er?
Sam: Sein Name ist Henry Igel.
Sue: Können wir ihn besuchen?
Sam: Heute nicht. Er schläft. Wir können ihn im April besuchen. Er schläft von Oktober bis April.
Sue: Schön. Dann können wir ihn im April besuchen.

Visitenkarte: Henry Igel
Adresse: Nußbaum-Haus

Seite 14 Winter
An diesem Morgen weckt Sue Sam! Warum ...?

Sue: Wach auf, Sam, es schneit!
Sam: Was?
Sue: Wach auf, es schneit!
Sam: Was? Es schneit? Ach, das sind Federn! Es schneit gar nicht.
Sue: In Ordnung, in Ordnung!

Seite 15 Sieh aus dem Fenster! Es schneit!

Sue: Aber schau nur! Es schneit im Garten. Schau!
Sam: Hurra! Schnee, richtiger Schnee. Laß uns skilaufen.
Sue: Nein, nicht skilaufen. Ich möchte einen Schneemann bauen.
Sam: Wo ist mein Pullover? Wo ist mein Anorak?
Sue: Dein Pullover ist im Schrank. Dein Anorak hängt am Schrank.
Sam: Wo sind meine Skier?
Sue: Deine Skier sind unter dem Schrank. Wo ist meine Hose?
Sam: Deine Hose ist unter dem Bett.

Seite 16 Sam fährt Ski, und Sue baut einen Schneemann. Die Sonne scheint.

Sam: Ich fahre gern Ski! Heute scheint die Sonne. Ich mag die Sonne.
Sue: Ich mag meinen Schneemann! Und ich mag die Sonne.

Der Schneemann

Sieh meinen Schneemann an, rund und dick.
Er hat einen Schal und eine Wollmütze.
Steine als Augen, eine Möhre als Nase,
Stöcke als Arme und Stiefel für seine Zehen.

Seite 17 Du liebe Zeit! Sam ist hingefallen. Er hat sich am Bein verletzt.

Sam: Aua, mein Bein!
Sue: Ach herrje! Gehen wir zum Doktor!

Sam: Ich mag es, auf dem Schlitten zu fahren. Danke, daß du mich ziehst.
Sue: Ich ziehe dich gerne. Gehen wir nach Hause.

Seite 18 Die Bären verbringen einen ruhigen Tag zu Hause.

Sam: Ich mag das Feuer. Es ist warm!
Sue: Ja, es ist kalt draußen, und es schneit. Wie geht es deinem Bein, Sam?
Sam: Danke, Sue, gut. Aber ich habe Durst. Kann ich bitte etwas zu trinken haben?
Sue: Etwas zu trinken? Ja, was möchtest du haben? Früchtetee oder ein Zitronengetränk mit Honig?
Sam: Früchtetee? Nein, danke. Aber ich mag Zitrone und Honig. Ein Zitronengetränk mit Honig bitte.

Seite 19 Rezept: Zitronengetränk mit Honig

1 Tasse Wasser, 2 Teelöffel Honig, 1 Zitrone

Erhitze das Wasser.
Gib 2 Löffel Honig in die Tasse.
Schneide die Zitrone in zwei Hälften. Presse sie aus.

Gieße den Saft in die Tasse.
Gieße das heiße Wasser über den Honig und den Zitronensaft.
Rühre alles um. Mmh. Das schmeckt!

Seite 20/21

Frühling
März, April, Mai
Sommer
Juni, Juli, August
Herbst
September, Oktober, November
Winter
Dezember, Januar, Februar

Seite 22 Frühling

Sue and Sam frühstücken zusammen.
Schau auf den Kalender – der 1. April!

Sue: Guten Morgen, Sam.
Sam: Guten Morgen, Sue, komm her und frühstücke.
Sue: Ich bin durstig.
Sam: Möchtest du Tee oder Kakao?
Sue: Tee, bitte.
Sam: Hier, bitte. Bist du hungrig?
Sue: Ja, ich bin hungrig. Wo sind die Bärenflocken?
Sam: Die Bärenflocken? Hier sind sie.
Sue: Oh, ein Vogel!
Vogel: April! April! Fang mich!
Sue: Was für eine Überraschung! Ein Vogel! Laß uns den Vogel fangen!

Seite 23 Plötzlich flog ein Vogel zum Fenster herein. Sue und Sam sind wirklich überrascht. Aber wo ist der Vogel jetzt? Sue and Sam suchen ihn.

Sam: Ist er auf dem Schrank?
Sue: Nein, dort ist er nicht.
Sam: Hinter dem Schrank?
Sue: Nein, dort ist er nicht. Sieh unter dem Sofa nach.
Sam: Nein, dort ist er nicht.
Sue: Sieh nur, er ist in deinem Rucksack!
Sam: Hurra, ich habe ihn. Komm mit, laß uns nach draußen gehen.
Sue: Ja, gehen wir in den Garten.

Seite 24 Es ist ein wunderschöner Frühlingstag. Die Bären und der Vogel sind im Garten.

Sam: Kannst du mir bitte beim Säen helfen.
Sue: Nein, ich möchte auf die Schaukel gehen. Der Vogel kann dir helfen.
Sam: Komm her, Vogel. Bitte hilf mir.
Vogel: In Ordnung. Gib mir die Samen.
Sam: In Ordnung, zunächst einige Karotten hierher. Danke. Dann einige Radieschen dorthin.
Vogel: Dann hier ein paar Bohnen.

Seite 25 Sue ist auf der Schaukel. Sie schaukelt gern.

Sue: Sam, bitte stoße mich an.
Sam: In Ordnung. Auf geht's.
Sue: Danke, Sam. Hui. Schaukeln macht Spaß.

Wie gefällt es dir, hoch hinauf zu schaukeln?
Hoch hinauf in den blauen Himmel?
Oh, ich denke, es ist das größte Vergnügen,
das ein Kind haben kann.
(Robert Louis Stevenson)

Seite 26 Die Hasen möchten ihre Eier im Garten verstecken. Sue, Sam und Henry Igel helfen ihnen.

Hase: Hallo, Sue und Sam. Wir möchten die Eier verstecken!
Sam: Können wir euch helfen?
Sue: Ja, laßt uns ein rotes Ei unter dem Busch verstecken.
Hase: Ein blaues Ei hinter den Blumen.
Sam: Ein orangefarbenes Ei neben den Bohnen.
Henry: Ein gelbes Ei und ein lila Ei im Gras.

Seite 27

Hase: Und noch ein gelbes Ei unter dem Baum.
Henry: Ein orangefarbenes Ei unter der Schaukel.
Sue: Ein lila Ei in den Blumen.
Sam: Und ein rotes Ei auf dem Baum, im Vogelnest.
Hasen: O ja. Oben auf dem Baum! Hier ist ein leeres Nest.
Sue: Das ist eine gute Idee!
Sam: Auf geht's, Henry.
Hasen: Fertig! Wir danken euch allen.
Sue: Hurra, die Körbe sind leer!

Seite 28 Sommer

Sue and Sam sind auf dem Zeltplatz. Sie möchten schwimmen gehen. Henry kommt sie besuchen.

Sue: So! Das Zelt ist aufgebaut! Nun, wo ist mein Badeanzug?
Sam: Hier ist meiner – aber wo ist meine Sonnenbrille?

Sue: Und meine Schwimmflossen? Und meine Sonnencreme?
Henry: Hallo, Sam, was macht ihr hier?
Sam: Oh, hallo, Henry. Wir zelten.
Sue: Schwimmst du gerne, Henry? Wir gehen jetzt schwimmen.
Henry: Nein, ich schwimme nicht gern, aber ich kann mitkommen und euch zuschauen.
Sue: In Ordnung, gehen wir. Und dann machen wir ein Picknick.
Henry: In Ordnung, ich mag Picknicks.

Seite 29 Nach dem Schwimmen sind die Bären und Henry hungrig. Sie mögen Picknicks. Sie mögen keine Bienen.

Sue: Ich habe jetzt Hunger. Laßt uns picknicken.
Sam: Und ich bin durstig. Ich möchte etwas zu trinken. Was hast du dabei, Sue?
Sue: Früchtetee und Limonade.
Sam: O, nein! Keinen Früchtetee! Ich möchte gern Limonade.
Sue: Ich habe ein paar Tomaten und ein Käsesandwich. Und zwei Sandwiches mit Honig und drei Äpfel. Was möchtest du, Henry?
Henry: Ich mag gern Äpfel. Einen Apfel, bitte.
Sue: Und du, Sam?
Sam: Ein Käsesandwich, bitte. Ich mag Käse. Danke.
Sue: Und ich mag Tomaten. Oh, eine Biene. Weg da!
Henry: Weg da, Biene! Ich kann Bienen nicht ausstehen.

Siehst du nicht, ich bin eine Biene,
Ich bin eine vielbeschäftigte Biene!
Ich mag Honig, und ich mag Tee.
Ich bin eine vielbeschäftigte Biene!

Seite 30 Sam angelt gern, aber Henry and Sue möchten Minigolf spielen.

Sue: Laßt uns Minigolf spielen.
Sam: Nein, ich möchte angeln gehen. Ich möchte einen Fisch zum Abendessen.
Henry: Aber ich mag Minigolf. Ich kann mit dir spielen, Sue.
Sue: Komm, Henry, du kannst anfangen. Hier ist der Ball. Zuerst spielen wir durch den Tunnel.
Henry: Eins ... ! Zwei ... durch den Tunnel. Drei ... im Loch! Hurra!
Sue: Gut, jetzt bin ich an der Reihe. Eins, zwei ... im Loch!
Henry: Du bist sehr gut. Versuchen wir jetzt die nächste Bahn. Den Hügel hinauf.
Sue: Versuche es noch einmal, Henry.
Henry: Da! Den Hügel hinauf. Hurra. Er ist im Loch. Nun bist du dran, Sue.
Sue: In Ordnung, den Hügel hinauf. Eins ... , zwei ... , drei ... , vier ...! Hurra, er ist im Loch.

Seite 31

Henry: In Ordnung. Nun den Hügel hinunter. Ich bin dran.
Sue: O je! Der Ball ist im Wasser! Komm, laß uns nach Sam sehen.

1, 2, 3, 4, 5, einst fing ich einen lebenden Fisch,
6, 7, 8, 9, 10, dann ließ ich ihn wieder frei.
Warum hast du ihn freigelassen?
Weil er mir in den Finger gebissen hat!
In welchen Finger hat er gebissen?
In diesen kleinen Finger der rechten Hand!

Seite 32 Am Abend sitzen Sam, Sue und Henry am Lagerfeuer. Der Fisch brät auf dem Feuer.

Sue: Das ist ein großer Fisch, Sam. Ich bin hungrig.
Henry: Fisch zum Abendessen. Ich mag Fisch. Ich zelte gern.
Sue: Ja, Zelten macht Spaß. Hey, seht euch die Sterne an.
Sam: Ich kann euch ein Lied über die Sterne singen.

Funkel, funkel, kleiner Stern,
Wie läßt du mich staunen.
Hoch oben über der Welt
Wie ein Diamant am Firmament.
Funkel, funkel, kleiner Stern,
Wie läßt du mich staunen.

Seite 33 Die Bären sind müde. Der Tag war wunderschön. Der Mond und die Sterne leuchten. Euch allen eine gute Nacht.

Sam: Ich bin müde. Das war ein wunderschöner Tag.
Sue: Ja, ich bin auch müde. Der Fisch war sehr gut, Sam.
Sam: Wo ist mein Schlafsack?
Sue: Im Zelt. Schaut euch den Mond an. Er leuchtet.
Sam: Ja, es ist wundervoll. Henry, bist du müde? ... Henry?
Henry: Ja. Allen eine gute Nacht. Schlaft gut.
Sue: Schlaft gut. Gute Nacht.

rain
umbrella
anorak
leaf
grass
six
cheese
hole
nose
hand
arm
pants
girl
seven
lemon
bees
red
white
yellow
blue
green
flowers
tree
house
bush
sunglasses
eight